About The Author!

Hello, I'm Pasha Rana. Nice To Meet You! At 29 years old I'm pretty proud of the life I've been able to create for myself. After successfully launching online businesses, I now help others be more successful in theirs. I'm passionate about that. I build successful marketing companies on the Internet. I guess above all I'm a creator. I love building stuff that people will love. I consult marketing companies to expand their revenue streams. Love helping others achieve their goals: financial or personal. That's what I'm most passionate about and gets me excited every week. I'm a strict believer that happiness is the highest form of success. If I can make you a little bit happier in this life than my hard work was worth it! I've Helped Teach Many...

YOU'RE NEXT!

ALL RIGHTS RESERVED

DISCLAIMERS

Table of Contents

1	Quick Introduction.
2	Develop a Strong and Powerful Mindset.
3	The First Step For Network Marketing Success.
4	Simple & Proven Money Formula.
5	Why You're Not Earning Enough.
6	How To Offer your Deepest Transformation.
7	What's Next?

Chapter 1

Quick Introduction.

First of all, you need to know that there are really only 2 ways for you to make money online -- which is either by selling your own product, or selling other people's products.

If you think about it, selling your own product should be the best option, right?

However, that's far from the truth and is also what most people fail to understand! You see, in order for you to sell your own product, you must have these TWO issues sorted out first:

- ## Your product has to be really amazing.

The fact is, there are hundreds or even thousands of similar products to yours for a consumer to choose from – so your product has got to have its own "secret recipe" to stand out from the crowd. Otherwise, it's not going to get the attention.

- ## You got to master internet marketing!

The point is having an awesome product is just one part of the equation. The second part is, being able to sell it online (profitably) and that means you MUST have the following:

A converting, professionally-designed website.

A great web copy or a video sales letter to do the selling job for you

Then what about product fulfillment, follow up marketing, building your brand and so on?

It all needs taking care of. If you're just starting out, you could end up losing a lot of money by trying to sell your own product and worse still, emotionally drained of not seeing any results for months!

So what's the secret to getting started and making some money online?

It lies in promoting someone else's products and earning a commission! This is called affiliate marketing. If you want to get started quickly, even as fast as making money online by NEXT WEEK, you should be promoting affiliate programs; because they're already proven to convert well.

The product creators have already developed an awesome product and tested that their website is able to convert the visitors aka, it converts traffic into sales!

What type of products should you go on to sell?

My immediate response would be information products like courses, software, eBooks, etc., simply because of these THREE reasons:

- Usually, you can earn a very high commission, as much as 100% because the product creator/owner has almost zero cost to his business.

- It's VERY EASY to get yourself started

- It usually converts better if it's presented to the right prospects because information products solve a "how to" problem, where, people are willing to pay for the information that they need.

Note: If you're completely new to affiliate marketing, I've written a separate PDF called "Quick Guide To Affiliate Marketing" that will bring you up to speed. You can view that here.

http://pasharana.eliteprofitsystem.com/Guide

Chapter 2

Develop a Strong and Powerful Mindset.

A few years before I got into internet marketing, I was given a set of cassette tapes that featured the speaking of a philanthropist called John Kehoe. It was called "Mind Power".

It's kind of similar to Tony Robbins stuff that you may be familiar with.

Anyway, that was probably the first big turning point which lead me on my path outside of 'society's box' and into the life of my dreams.

For me to attempt to summarise what I learnt in 'Mind Power' in this short chapter here wouldn't do it justice, but I'll do my best to share with you my thoughts on mindset.

Not everything is from 'Mind Power' as I've developed my own thinking over the years (I'm 29 now).

To me the simple mindset fundamentals that you need to adopt to have the life of your dreams are:

- Know exactly what you want (these must be your dreams, not things that others want for you, or things you think that you should want).

- Believe whole heartedly that you can achieve your dreams, so much so that nobody or nothing can stop you from believing in yourself and your ability to get there. Barriers to a strong self belief include:

- Lack of results: This is simply a challenge to overcome, it just means you haven't had results YET. If you keep working your plan, and perhaps adapt when there may be slight holes in it, then you will get there.

- Lack of support from others: This is often due to lack of belief in themselves and you cannot afford to let it dampen your own self belief in anyway. Make sure you surround yourself with people who are positive influences on your life, and preferably have people that you mix with that you look up to and wish to emulate.

- Have a strategy in place that you are following on a daily basis to get closer every day towards the fulfilment of your dreams.

- Develop a strong passion for learning, and be extremely positive about tricky challenges.

- Eat well balanced meals and exercise on a daily basis. Preferably find a sport or something that you enjoy and makes you want to keep doing it regularly. Even better if one of your dreams involves exercise to get there.

- Love your life as it is now and enjoy the challenge and the journey.

The hardest thing for most people seems to be to do with self belief. It leads people to procrastinate, to not work towards their goals with enthusiasm and determination (instead with scepticism and lack of belief, ready to give up at early obstacles).

When I was going through Mind Power, John Kehoe suggested affirmations. He said that if you repeat the same statement out loud every single day for 5 minutes a day for 90 days, you will reprogram your subconscious mind to take on that new belief.

Being an extremely shy guy at the time, I took on the following affirmation:

"I'm extremely self confident and I love taking risks"

I also had:

"Every day in every way I'm getting better, better and better"

I had a couple more and also imprinted other beliefs on my brain over the year and beyond.

The key was that I was ready to not settle for the mindset that I had at the time. I purposely reprogrammed my brain to believe in itself.

It's interesting how many people I see in society that become self-fullfilling prophecies of themselves. "Oh I can't do this", "Oh that's easy for you, but I could never do that!", "I'm never going to meet a great man/woman", "I'm to stupid to xyz", etc.

It's so easy to say negative things to yourself all the time. Why not consciously start changing the words that go on inside your head to positive ones?

For me, I've become a self-fulfilling prophecy based on the beliefs I imprinted on myself many years ago. People who knew me since I was younger than 22 can't believe where I am now, it has been a total transformation – nothing less.

And you can have it too.

Think of imprinting like this. If you take a large bucket of water and drop a drop of red dye into it each day, sooner or later the bucket of water will become red.

The same is true of yourself belief system. If you do the 5 minutes a day of out loud affirmations (each affirmation must be for 5 minutes each, so only start with 2 or 3), and you keep doing it for 90 days, your mind will take on that new belief system and help you move towards your goals on a subconscious level.

One last thing I wanted to mention is that in my opinion it is easier to work hard with

passion towards a goal when it has a deeper purpose or meaning. By deeper purpose, I mean working hard to serve something beyond you. There is nothing at all wrong with wanting to get rich, wanting to have a family and so forth, however beyond that, when you have those things, you'll probably find that the things that drive you further are what you can do for other people including family, friends, community and so forth.

Anyway, I'm no John Kehoe or Tony Robbins, but I hope that I've done enough in this very short chapter to convince you to upgrade your mindset as the life of your dreams is at stake.

Note: I've written a separate PDF called "Vision & Goals" that will bring you up to speed. You can view that here.

http://pasharana.eliteprofitsystem.com/Goals

Chapter 3

The First Step For Network Marketing Success.

Today I want to share with you the secret to success in network marketing. Every day people ask me, from all over the world, Pasha, what do I have to do in order to become a network marketing professional?

What do I have to do to get to the top? What's the secret to success? And of course, anybody who's been involved in business for any period of time understands that there's no one absolute thing; there's no shortcut to success. But I will tell you this. The beginning of the journey, the thing that's required in order for you to unlock all of the other things that you must unlock in order to become a network marketing professional, that's what I'm gonna share with you today.

Okay? So if you're looking for the secret, if you're looking for that one thing, if there was one thing that you had to do in order to go to the top, I'm gonna give you that one thing.

what I want to talk to you about today, and here's the secret.

Make a decision. A real decision that you're not gonna look right, you're not gonna look left, you're looking straight forward. There is no retreat. There are no other options. You're going to the top. You're gonna go to the top of the mountain. They're gonna see you waving from the top of the mountain or dead on the side of the road on the path to that summit because you're not coming back. That that moment when you burn your bridges, that moment when you

eliminate all your escape plans and all your Plan Bs and Plan Cs and Plan Ds. The thing that gets in the way of most of your success in network marketing is you have too many other options.

One of the greatest things that happened to me in network marketing is I didn't have any place else to go. I didn't have a lot of skills and talent and ability.

So I was forced to go down this road because of a lack of options. But some of you have so many options that you still haven't made a decision. Now understand, in my first four years of network marketing, I thought I had made a decision. I thought – if somebody asked me, "Are you committed?" "Yes, I'm committed.

Look at me. I'm working hard." "Are you going to the top?" "Oh, absolutely." But there was still stuff that could knock me off track.

If I lost a strong part of my organization, fell away, or quit, or went to another company, or something, that would discourage me deeply, and it would knock me off track for months. If I didn't hit a rank when I thought I was going to, I was just so upset about that. If I was disappointed or if I was embarrassed, of if I had some level of expectation not met, I would question my decision, and I would question my ability to be here.

And here's the thing. Guess what the world is really good at? The world is really good at saying, "Yeah, I'll try it. I'll give it a try. We'll give it a go. We'll see what happens. We'll cross our fingers. We'll hope for the best. We'll sign up for network marketing, and if something goes well, then maybe we'll continue."

So you're totally being tossed around by external circumstance instead of making a decision. A decision, a real decision says "I'm going. I'm going to the top."

A decision says, "It doesn't matter what other people in my local market are doing. I'm gonna do what's necessary to go to the top." A decision says, "I don't need training. I'll find the training necessary to do what I need to do in this profession because I'm going to the top." See what I mean? I don't need support. I don't need an upline. I don't need magical recognition. I don't need somebody to pat me on the head. I don't need a circle of friends to support me. I made a decision
– a decision, not a wish, not a hope for, not an "I'll give it a try".

I made a decision.

If there's the key to success, in my opinion, that would be that you once and for all make a decision, no matter how the person around you reacts, how the customers react to your product, how your prospects react to your presentation.

That doesn't matter. Here's what matters. If somebody in your company has gone all the way to the top that means you can too. There's not barrier as far as your educational requirements. There's no barrier based upon your age or your gender, or your race, your color, your skill level. There are no barriers there.

You can learn this. These skills are available to you. The talents and abilities necessary to become a network marketing professional are within your reach. If you make a decision, all the obstacles fall away. They become invisible. But until you make a decision, every single obstacle, every single tiny little bump in the road will seem
like Mount Everest and you cannot get past it. Do you understand what I'm saying to you?

If your decision is real, the objections fall away. If the decision is not real, you get discouraged, you get pushed around, you get all these different things happen to you on a regular basis.

Now you have an opportunity and a chance today to make a decision, for real. And, why do I do these shows? Why do I share these ideas for the network marketing profession? Because I've been where you've been and I've done what you've done, and I've had the struggle, and I've had the success. And I want to see you have a breakthrough.

I know you're tired of crawling through network marketing. I know that you know that you have more potential than this, and you have more ability than this. I know that you're tough on yourself and hard on yourself. And most of the pain will go away when you make the decision.

Now, the hardest part is making it, for real. But once you make the decision, most of the pain falls away because your options and your choices and all these different roads are now closed to you, and you have the one road in front of you, which is becoming a network marketing professional and serving the people that you have
the opportunity to connect with and provide value with, with your products and services and with your opportunity, moving forward on that road instead of being distracted like the world wants us to be, in a thousand different directions.

So make a decision. The world will be yours if you make a decision.

I hope you make your decision today.

Now let's go tell the world.

Chapter 4

Simple & Proven Money Formula

[Traffic] x [Conversion rate] x [$ per customer] x [# of transactions] = Your Paycheck

I didn't invent the above formula, it is a modification on a formula I read in a book by Brad Sugars few years ago and it is true for all businesses, including offline ones.

I'll give you an example of how this formula is calculated in affiliate marketing terms:

Let's say you own an affiliate website that promotes dog training products.

Traffic = 2000 visitors per day

Conversion rate = 0.37% (ie 1 in every 270 visitors to your website buys something)

$ per customer = $24.37 (ie the average commission you earn is $24.37)

# of transactions = 1.4 (ie customers usually buy 1 product from you, but some people opt into your mailing list and buy more products from you in the long run).

Therefore the amount you make from this website per day =

2000 x 0.37% x 24.37 x 1.4 = $252.47/day

Question: That's pretty obvious, why is that formula so important?

Answer: It may be obvious to some, but not to everyone. Also most people wind up having problems in one or more of those 4 major areas and if you don't pay attention it is easy to have holes in your marketing that you don't even see.

Bottom line is, you need to know your numbers when it comes to each of those 4 areas, particularly traffic and conversion rates.

Also, by keeping this formula in mind at all times in your marketing you can help prevent yourself becoming too heavily focussed on any one of those 4 areas.

Here are a few examples:

Someone might own a website that gets 1000 visitors per day, but makes no sales. The things that I advise are to do with conversion rates:

- Look at where the traffic is coming from... is it relevant? Are you advertising using popups on irrelevant websites? Are you optimizing for search engine keywords that are just not relevant enough for the product you are promoting?

- Look at the pages that are getting the most traffic and how people are getting there. What keywords are they typing in? What are they thinking and are your affiliate links placed in an obvious enough manner? Do they look credible? Is the product you are promoting credible?

Question: Do people really buy online?

Answer: Making money online is not rocket science, and it is not done by scamming people.

Hundreds of millions of people buy online every day because they are looking for information and/or specific products and buying online makes it easier for them than having to leave their houses or towns. Many people live in small towns and can't get fast access to products in physical locations anyway.

Also, some people are more affluent than others too. If you get 100 visitors per day to your website, chances are at least 5% of them will earn over 100k per year, and a decent lot more will earn over 50k per year.

You only need to convert at 1% or even less to make a good amount of money from a website. You yourself have probably bought something online before, if not, perhaps you know people who have.

Example of The Money Formula

Now that I've answered a few commonly asked questions, I'll continue by giving you a more detailed example of the money formula (based on the numbers from the earlier example).

Imagine that the 2000 visitors per day to the dog training website are broken down into the various pages like this:

Page a: 100 visitors per day
Page b: 20 visitors per day
Page c: 80 visitors per day
Pages d-z: 1800 visitors per day

Now, let's say the conversion rates are as follows:

Page a: 2% (i.e. 2% of people who visit this webpage buy a product you recommend)

Page b: 10%

Page c: 2%

Pages d-z: 0.1%

Overall then, your conversion rate is: 0.37%

I magine you promote a couple of products on your website and the average $ commission made = $24.37 (after fees etc)

Also you have a newsletter signup box, and as a result you often make multiple sales to the same people leading your average number of transactions to be 1.4 transactions per customer.

Back to the conversion rate above, at that conversion rate (0.37%), it takes you 270 visitors to your website per sale that you make. Sound familiar?

I see affiliates getting even worse conversion rates than that. It's not always bad, it depends on how many visitors you get, but as you can see from the above conversion rates, not all pages on your website will convert at the same rate.

This means that you could add another 100 pages to your website, but they might only convert at 0.1%. It isn't just about adding pages, you need to remember that with most of the pages you add to your website that you must select keywords that not only get good traffic numbers searching for them, but also keywords that are likely to convert well to sales and you need to set up your landing page so that it is likely to convert well.

Question: But wait... why do all the pages convert at different rates?

Answer: Not every page converts the same

Not all traffic converts the same either (perhaps pages d-z are attracting low quality unrelated traffic).

Low quality traffic is when you get visitors to your website but they aren't at all interested in what you are trying to promote to them.

For example: Well if someone types 'golden retriever' into google, and they find your golden retriever page on your website, and you are promoting a dog training product... then you might find that many of those people are not interested in your offer as they were looking for something else. Perhaps they are looking for pictures of golden retrievers.

However if someone searches for 'Golden retriever training' or 'stop dog aggression' or better yet 'review of DOG TRAINING PRODUCT NAME' (where 'dog training product name' is replaced by an actual name of a dog training product that you are promoting), then the conversion rates may be a LOT higher because these people typing these phrases into the search engines are actually looking for dog training information and may be willing to pay money for a product.

Another example of low quality traffic is if you are doing twitter marketing and promoting a dog training product to a bunch of people who are just in no way interested (better to start a dog lovers twitter community than get any old followers).

There are many more examples.

Now I could go on for quite some time with this above example, but I don't want to confuse what is a relatively simple concept.

One last point I wanted to make is you only need one source of traffic.

Yes there are many and you can focus on more and more of them later, but you only need 1 for the formula to work (e.g. Search engine traffic, pay per click traffic, media traffic, links from blogs etc, Google content network traffic, and so forth). The reason I'm making this point is that some people get too hung up on trying to get traffic from everywhere that they neglect the other parts of the formula, such as conversion rates.

Just remember, you don't want a zero anywhere in the formula.

Chapter 5

Why You're Not Earning Enough

If you are passionate about the work you do, but
your business isn't bringing in the kind of income you expected, you're not alone. My research with hundreds of business owners shows that only about 20% of heart-centered business owners consider themselves to be earning enough.

That means about 80% of business owners are underearning.
Since you're reading this report, you know in your heart that doing "okay" or "scraping by" isn't cutting it.

I'm on a MISSION to put an end to this.

That's what this chapter is all about.

I'm on a mission to end undercharging and underearning, and that's what this report is here to help you with!

I meet with mission-oriented business owners all the time who are not charging enough to have an income that sustains them. And it breaks my heart to see these kindred spirits suffering – and not doing the work they're here to do.

If you have a gap between where you are and where you want to be with money and wealth, then this just might be the most important message you've ever received.

- Say goodbye to underearning and undercharging.

- Say goodbye to the fear and stress you have around money.

- Say hello to ease and joy as you run your business, making all of the money you desire.

Here's "why" you're not earning enough:

It's shockingly simple.

The biggest problem

I see is that people are **undercharging** for their services. Here's what I mean. If you're doing everything you can to get clients to pay you
for an hour of work or a few sessions in a package, that's the slow boat that never gets you to a financially viable business.

It is a common misperception that **charging as little as possible** is an effective strategy for attracting new clients.

The problem is this: Instead of focusing on solutions to big problems, you're trying to sell a bit of your time to clients.

This has the unfortunate side effect of repelling clients who are looking for someone to provide a complete SOLUTION to an urgent problem or need.

The secret to breaking free from "underearning"

If you are a **coach, holistic practitioner, consultant, healer, trainer, author, therapist,** or a **business owner** with services that make a positive difference AND you haven't yet gotten to the income you want, you're about to learn a critical strategy that allows you to **work less, earn more, and make a bigger difference.**

This isn't going to be about abstract wealth consciousness (although I think money mindsets are important). This is actually something very practical.

The strategy is this:

Offer "high-ticket" packages that deliver a big result that solves an urgent problem or pain that your clients have.

Doing this immediately shifts you from chasing low-paying clients to being attractive to clients who are highly motivated and value the transformation you offer.

These clients will pay anywhere from $1,000 to $10,000 (or more) for valuable results.

The best thing about this: You only have to work with a small number of clients to make a great income.

Focus on value, not $ per hour

Offering premium packages helps you get out of the trading-time-for-dollars model.

Because clients pay you for the massive value you provide, instead of haggling over your hourly rate.

This ONE change in your business – shifting from low-end packages to high-end packages – changes EVERYTHING.

Note: I've written a separate PDF called "Premium Manifesto 2016" that will bring you up to speed. You can view that here.

http://pasharana.eliteprofitsystem.com/Manifesto

You've probably heard about "high-ticket" or "high-end" packages or offerings.

I call these high-end offerings "Premium Packages." And these are the best cure for undercharging and underearning.

Here's why: Premium Packages are all about providing your
clients with big results and a deep level of transformation.
And when you do that, you are well paid for your experience
and knowledge.

Here's how I define Premium Packages: A package of services (and sometimes products) that delivers a highly desirable result or transformation in the most effective way possible.

Premium Packages = amazing
transformation (for your clients)
+ generous compensation (for you).

If you offer services that help people with their wealth, their health, their relationships, or their personal and spiritual growth – then Premium Packages will work in your business.

In this report, I'll show you how offering Premium Packages is the easiest way for your business and your income to take off, and at the same time, how you can serve your clients in a massive way – all from a place of integrity and generosity.

This is your opportunity to create a business that is thriving financially, while doing what you love.

So what exactly is a Premium Package?

Here's the basic idea behind Premium Packages.

It starts with designing and offering packages in the $1,000 to $10,000 range, or even more.

However, it's not just about raising your prices.

It's about creating packages that deliver a deep level of transformation for your client. Not just a band-aid, but the big result they really wanted when they came to you.

This would radically change the world, if we all did our best work with clients, instead of just an hour or two of work that barely helps people with the big needs and results they really are clamoring for.

It's my intention that in reading this, you can learn from my hard-earned lessons and accelerate your learning, so you don't have to make the same mistakes I have.

Undercharging Seriously Harms Your Business

This may not have occurred to you, but undercharging is actually costing your business.

Here are 5 big problems you run into when you mainly provide low cost offerings to clients:

1. **Short client engagements** (so you're always needing new clients)
2. Clients get **minimal results** (it takes time to get results)
3. Clients **don't value you** (they don't show up, do the work, etc)
4. Need a **lot of clients** (since the income from each client is low)
5. A new client makes **little difference to your income**

I want to break down why going "low-end" creates a lot of work for you and will practically guarantee that you will keep your income low.

The "wrong way" (what doesn't work)

I want to show you 3 typical things you might be doing in your business now that don't work very well, and keep you underearning.

SCENARIO #1: Offering Single sessions
- Example - $75 per session
- **Problem**: You need to sell 50-100 sessions EVERY MONTH to earn a
good living. That's very difficult.

SCENARIO #2: Offering a bunch of low cost items .
- Example: $47 audio recordings
- **Problem**: You need a huge list (10,000 people or more) to sell a lot of these. Usually people are generating very little income with these items.

SCENARIO #3: Low-Cost Group Programs
- Example: $197 per person to be in your group
- **Problem**: You have to be constantly marketing to get people into your group. And these small fees barely add up.

A lot of clients who come to me are offering to work with their clients on a single session basis. Or maybe it's a package of 3 or 4 sessions.

The basic idea is this: Lets say you offer one session at a time, and let's say you charge $75. That means that you need to work with 50-100 clients a month to generate a pretty good income.

Here's the problem:

• That's a lot of work to deliver your service.
• That's a lot of work administratively to keep track and schedule all the appointments, not to mention managing the accounting and billing too.
• And more troubling than anything else – that's a lot of work on the sales and marketing side of things to generate the amount of

interest you need in order to work with this many people.

That is definitely the hard road to success.

You have to continually be spending time marketing to bring in new people for these short engagements.

Instead, you could be spending the same amount of effort (or less) on landing a smaller number of higher end clients where the engagements last longer, your clients are more committed, and you are getting paid a good amount of money.

WARNING: Charging by the hour limits your income.

Chapter 6

How To Offer your Deepest Transformation.

**So here's the secret to creating an amazing business
with Premium Packages: Offer your Deepest Transformation.**

When I am talking about a Premium Package, I am talking about you creating an offering of service or a program that is specifically designed to create deep, lasting or extremely desirable transformation.

People are willing to pay more when you take them to the result they want, rather than just offering a band-aid for their problem.

The first step in offering Premium Packages is to have a compelling ultimate result – something that people have a lot of natural desire for at that particular moment in time. The kind of offering I'm talking about will help solve an urgent problem someone is having that they would be willing to invest a premium for.

It's about offering and doing your best work that you can be really proud of. I know for me, offering Premium Packages gave me the incentive and that extra nudge to continually be committed to my craft and getting better and better at what I do. It was the rallying cry I needed to be the best that I can be.

I also know that in order for me to be of ultimate service to people, I need to be their coach or mentor for a period of time, which allows me to truly bring everything I have to offer to that client. We all know that to create real, meaningful change or produce truly desirable result in a business, in someone's health or love life, or in their personal growth (in any important area, really), it takes time because the day you plant the seed is not the day you pick the fruit.

Simplify Your Business: Only Offer Premium Packages

So here's the next thing I would love for you to know about Premium Packages:

When you simplify your business and design your business model to be attracting and enrolling the majority of your clients into Premium Packages...... you wind up making more money and working a lot less.

A lot of my clients are moms who can't or don't want to work a lot.

A lot of my clients want to travel or live a full life.

And they want to make a difference in the world without needing to slave away by working too much and getting burnt out and overwhelmed.

Premium Packages are the antidote to burn out, too.

I was just talking to a new client of mine. He has simplified his business model to 10 clients at $16,000 per client. He doesn't want to do anything else. He wants to travel. He wants to have a life where he is not working 40-60 hours a week.

I remember looking at him as he came to this realization. His face lit up. All the pressure he was previously feeling disappeared. His shoulders relaxed.

It's a relief to know that you don't have to work a lot to make a huge impact with a small number of premium clients.

It seems contradictory to the message we often hear – work hard, do more.

Instead, what if you were to simply change your business model and begin to SIMPLIFY everything in your business by offering Premium Packages?

When you stop doing too much and simplify, you can get out of financial anxiety.

Plus you get to show up fully to do your best work, and you get to create deep and meaningful transformations.

Offer your Deepest Transformation

I am going to share with you how you're in position to make
**$1000, $5000 and $10,000 (total $16,000 per client) commissions over & over (not One Time) from the each sale
that is made for you.**

What if you can earn more money in 30-45 mins a day than most people make working full-time?

Does this sounds

To Good Too Be True?

Well, It's NOT

The system I'm about to reveal would let you do this.

With your permission, I'll give you simple & proven formula you can use to potenially make BIG MONEY in minutes a day.

Use it for a week and take the rest of the month off.

Using this system for a brief period of time on the days you decide to put in can be so easy.

This can take as little as 45 minutes a day or less.

And you can live a life that others can only dream of. Most people work 260 days a year and you can make BIG MONEY as little as in fews days a week.

Most people get 1-2 weeks of vacation, but you can take 1-2 weeks of vacation or more... each month.

This system is lot of fun, I know you'll love it.

Most people only make certain amount of money, but my proven system lets you make as much as you want. I'll show you how.

It's simple and most of the work is done for you.

Your friends will think you won the **"Lottery"**

Simplify Your Business
Offer Elite Profit System

Introducing The Only High-Ticket Residual Income Affiliate Program In the Industry Today!

Imagine if...

- You didn't need to write or produce any content
- You didn't need to create any membership program
- You didn't need to create any products to sell
- You didn't need to come up with your own free offer
- You didn't need to write any sales letters
- You didn't need to pay for hosting or an auto-responder
- You didn't need to send emails at all
- You didn't need to provide any customer service or follow up
- You didn't need to research for what products or affiliate programs to promote
- You didn't even need to learn internet marketing!

Heck, with this program, you don't need to do anything except for one simple task!

When you choose to use the Elite Profit System, **you will get an exact clone of our proven, successful business** with the potential to generate a passive income through it... and we'll handle absolutely *everything* for you.

To unlock the door to higher commissions of $1,000 – $10,000 per sale by promoting our large selection of backend products, events and done-for-you services, you will need to upgrade to one of our business programs listed below.

EPS Admin Fee: $100/Month – No Commissions

EPS Gold Membership Fee:

One Time $1000 – 100% Commissions

EPS Diamond Membership Fee:

One Time $5000 – 100% Commissions

EPS Elite Membership Fee:

One Time $10,000 – 100% Commissions

10 Sales on ALL THREE LEVELS = $160,000 TOTAL Monthly Residual Income.

A GRAND TOTAL OF $1,920,000.00/YEAR

Where To Find Clients For Your High-Ticket Online Business?

Ever since we added the 3 step formula to EPS, everyday people just like you have been able to make an extra $2000- $23,000 a month working only 30 minutes a day.

Let me share with you what exactly you'll be doing to make that much money with minimal effort.

Step 1.

Set up 3 toll free numbers. (Takes about 1 minute to do)
The staff will upload the messages for you to the numbers you chose.

Step 2.

Contact our lead source and have them run the advertising for you.
(Wait for messages to pour in to your inbox by hot prospects wanting more information)

Step 3.

Text message your prospects with your affiliate link and give your assigned sales agent the names and numbers of your prospects. (Sales agents will follow up with your prospects and close the sale for you).

AND..... YOU'RE DONE!

It's that simple.

Note: I've written a separate PDF called "Where To Find High-Paying Clients" that will bring you up to speed. You can view that here.

http://pasharana.eliteprofitsystem.com/Clients

How To Get Paid High-Ticket ($1000, $5000 and $10,000) Commissions over & over from the same amount of work and clients?

With Elite Profit System, once you make your first sale, a time-clock will start counting back from 30-zero days. Once your membership is expired, you'll have two 2 options to re-activate your membership level.

You may either pay from the profits to re-activate your membership
Or you simply make another sale and system will automatically
re-activate your membership level.

All clients in your downline will do the same and you'll receive these high-ticket commissions over & over each month without needing any extra work and without worrying to find new clients each month.

Lack of cash flow and profits is what holds back most businesses, specifically online business owners and network marketers.

Sometimes, the problem is lack of sales. Other times, the problem is just not making much profit per sale that can contribute to a decent and realistic income.

Most can do that but not everyone can recruit 1000 people per month in MLM or make 1000 affiliate product sales a month.

This is the "EVERY MAN BUSINESS"

In my 4 years of making money online I've found that it takes just as much 'work' to sell a $10 product as it does a $1,000 product.

What's this "Insanely Profitable" System is all about?

- **Make BIG RESIDUAL Income Fast!** (EPS was designed to help struggling marketers make a long lasting residual income without the headache of recruiting , selling or chasing anyone. You only need 10 people to make $160,000/month. (With EPS, just 10 average sales will make you $160k per month with a great potential to make $2 Million/Year. (Just 10 sales) THAT'S IT!!)

- **Done For you follow up system** (You don't have to learn how to create capture pages that convert. It's Done for you. You don't need to learn Email Marketing and complicated autoresponders systems. You don't need to learn how to write emails that build relationship and trust with your list. Our powerful system will send follow up emails to your prospects promoting your affiliate link without needing any effort from you.)

- **Weekly conference calls** (We will hold weekly conference calls for you to invite your prospects and we will help you close the deals)

- **Live Google Hangouts** (Top industry leaders will teach to how to build your EPS business)

- **Powerful Marketing tools and training** (Whether you're a seasoned affiliate marketer looking to expand your products and solutions portfolio or you're just starting your online business journey now, Our affiliate resources & tools will help you get there faster)

- **No Risk** (There is NO RISK on anyone who joins this program. Get ready for the ride of your life with this never done before concept..it's the perfect system where all members profit . This is literally the best high ticket residual based one of a kind no risk system on the net or anywhere else)

If you're someone with an UNSTOPPABLE entrepreneurial mindset who's open to making a 5-6 figure income from home, Click below to get started now... I can help!

GET STARTED HERE!
http://pasharana.eliteprofitsystem.com/GetStarted

Bonus #1 : FREE Upgrade To ELITE ULTRA ($10,000 Cash Value)

If You Take Action Today You'll Also Get the Following BONUS!

Upgrade To Elite Diamond within first 30 Days of Joining Elite Profit System and Get Free upgrade to Elite Ulra Level ($10,000 Bonus)

Bonus #2 : Your own Customised Blog

Blogging is very powerful, You'll get your own EPS customised blog, <u>similar to this one here</u>

LEARN MORE ABOUT ELITE PROFIT SYSTEM HERE!

www.pasharana.eliteprofitsystem.com/GetStarted

If you need to get started, Please email me

Email: info@pasharana.com

Where To Next?

Firstly, if you enjoyed this book then please pass this on to other people who you think may benefit from it. Perhaps you have a twitter list or friends who you think will gain value from this. I encourage you to pass it around by sending people to:

Share This Book
www.PashaRana.com

Next, make sure you watch this video...
www.pasharana.eliteprofitsystem.com/GetStarted

Elite Profit System Conference Call!
www.pasharana.eliteprofitsystem.com/CallReplay

All the best to your success!

Pasha Rana

Pasha Rana
President & C.E.O: The Pasha Group
Business Development Director:
(@ Elite Profit System Inc)
Email: info@pasharana.com
Website: www.PashaRana.com